Song
&
Spectacle

Song
&
Spectacle

Rachel Rose

HARBOUR PUBLISHING

Harbour Publishing Co. Ltd.
P.O. Box 219, Madeira Park, BC, V0N 2H0
www.harbourpublishing.com

Edited by Sam Green and Elaine Park
Cover art: "Midnight Flight" by Jorden and David Doody (2007, mixed media, 3.5' x 6')
Cover design: Anna Comfort O'Keeffe
Printed and bound in Canada

Harbour Publishing acknowledges financial support from the Government of Canada through the Canada Book Fund and the Canada Council for the Arts, and from the Province of British Columbia through the BC Arts Council and the Book Publishing Tax Credit.

Library and Archives Canada Cataloguing in Publication

Rose, Rachel, 1970–
    Song & spectacle / Rachel Rose.

Poems.
ISBN 978-1-55017-585-1

    I. Title.

PS8585.O7325S66 2012   C811'.54   C2012-904936-0

For Isabelle, always and all ways.

Contents

Ways to Begin a Poem

1.

Begin at the source. Open the book of thyself,
contentious one, thy book in four chapters, four scrolls.
Rise on your own yeast. Spill your villanelles'
hot vowels. You will not go
blind. Though imagine what you might see
if you did.

2.

Begin with a friend (a writer) playing a board game
at a party. Question: something found in a desk
that starts with J. His answer: Jizm. Haiku the difference
between men and women. Stray red leaf.

3.

Begin with seed, then. The way we touch each
other. Flipped: a car on fire after a game involving men
in padded suits. Brute mob drenched in fuel. Saltpeter.

4.

Fertilized papyrus
of undecipherable texts. Ink licked to language,
stanza after stanza of buttons popped. Terza rima
of nipples, navel, quilt washed in light.

5.

Outside bombs dismantle a station. Somewhere else
not here. Begin again, please. Pantoum com-
munion. To be written, to be folded into shapes
suited to the poem. Smell of a river waiting for salmon.

6.

Not here. Begin again, please. Pantoum: come
inside my body. Joy of song without words
suited to the poem. Smell of a river waiting for salmon.
Silhouette of your form against a torn white curtain.

7.

Poem of thy creases. O where have you been, sweet
reeking ballad monster? Pray
that tomorrow will know by heart
today. Begin by holding hands
under the table. A hip kisses a tambourine.
A troubadour is condemned for her troubles.
Our love meets in the ruins of a castle
full of ravens. We

8.

buy daffodils, we play the cello badly but with joy.
We grow yellow tomatoes. We let them cut us open,
we put children in the garden. Remembering the loneliness
of the lunch room, we decide not to have children.
If the form can be found, there may be salvation.
There are lilacs. Lilacs have form. It is quiet
but for the poem's gasp. We bone thrust until we bruise
apart. Naked in the kitchen, we slice chanterelles for dinner,
add a fistlump of butter, crushed sage. Fragrance enters
your hair. My own. Is there one god, or many? Evening star
sings forth a thousand more in the pale green mosque
of the sky. Stretch marks. Two lemons on a table. Still life.
Begin with the body, poisoned to save the body.
Tragicomedy. The form.

Willingness

The years have shown that there is no armor. There never was. The willingness to be wounded may be all we have to offer.

—DR. ABRAHAM VERGHESE

This morning I planned to dig manure into the garden,
but woke to a cold snap, each horse turd rimed with ice.
Still, I wouldn't go inside as the baby napped in her carriage,
mourning the brevity of my solitude
until my hands were numb.
In an hour, I'll wait at the corner for my son's bus,
wondering how long it's been since I've changed my tampon,
if the halibut's thawed, if I should've put the laundry through
instead of falling on the bed in the other room
coming, screaming alone into a bent pillow.
Perhaps it's these dark-at-four
November afternoons that sting my eyes,
the rain, the knowledge that I'll never be pregnant again.

The years have shown

I'll never again be doubly alive,
and no matter how hard I tried
to pay attention, each change appeared
as I was folding the small jumpers,
as I was wiping the plastic tray, fractured,
unwashed, not truly listening.
When did her hot foot outgrow
my hand?

She wakes, apricot-cheeked, and fits herself
to nurse. We sit this way for a long time
and nothing happens as she grows.
When I ask her if she's done
she shakes a tiny finger at me,

then pops off to explain,
"I can't really talk right now."

The bursts of joy
shrapnel, bringing me
to a crouch, and

there is no armor.
But a new one every spring!
The soup always simmering, a baby always
on my shoulder. That sweet spit milk,
my sour armpits, its tiny pursed lips,
and my love walking in
with anemones and dry cleaning.
Longing for a chance
to pay attention this time.

Also to live the ascetic life of a poet
in the mountains, books
my only company, a narrow bed,
my fire the size of the afternoon's gathered twigs.

There never was

time to be monogamous!
To know that grace, that serious marriage—
but sometimes music pulses from cafes
I long to enter
as I hurry home with my hot loaves, two
jugs of milk and

the willingness to be wounded.

Yes, the desire to love several countries,
to have familiar relationships with shopkeepers
on every continent. To live and die in this house,

growing the garden,
a dozen white chickens

may be all we have to offer.

There is no armor. Now I see. The bus coughs
my son free. His face holds the day's last light.
He runs spilling papers across the floor.
Her hands lift my shirt. Her teeth hurt.
There is no armor.
Let the ordinary days endure.

What We Heard About the Heart

We heard you like red wine,
dark chocolate, prefer iambic

pentameter to free verse. Our
specialists study your ailments: we call them

cardiologists, poets. We give your aches
the names of movie stars: *Angina, Arrhythmia, Tamponade.*

We hear you won't go on forever,
and that gives us pause.

Each of your two and a half billion beats
shapes our hours. Our tickers stutter

like firecrackers, pressed against the breasts
of lovers. In dance clubs, we hear your be-bop

with the bass thrum in our ears. Tough muscle:
we put our hands on you to swear the whole truth

and nothing but. We give you
a day of candies and roses,

frilled boxes, pink and labial. We vow to stay true.
Don't be still, my heart. Once,

before memory, you shocked us to life,
began the mystery. No one knows how. Sweet

heart: we ask for a generous span of beats.
We pray when you stop, you stop

in our sleep.

Heartsong

I heard I'm a lonely hunter. Don't believe it.
I'm the life of the party. Nor am I like a wheel:

You can mend me when I fail,
with stents, pacemakers.

To learn by me is to know by memory
for all your years. Come to my rooms, my chambers.

The Chinese proverb says *If I keep a green bough
in my heart, a singing bird will come.* Please don't

try this. I am the seat of metaphor. I am absolutely literal.
Aspirin soothes heartache. Try it.

Loyal? You bet your life. Use me hard,
 I'll grow stately, I'll last. I'm here for you,

I tell your time. Set to tick by an unknown shock,
I begin below the mother clock.

Without me, you're nothing. Clench of
systole to scarlet tulip, diastole of

anemone. Blue veined coral
wrist. Arterial. Knock-knock. I'm talking

to you. Once I was called a book. I held
all your feelings. Saint Augustine weighed me in hand.

I was divine with secrets.
Now I am secular, your faithful valve.

I work without vacation or sick leave.
I fear arrhythmias, lightning, bullets.

I am the red engine between your lungs:
I think I can. Chuff and spark, I go on.

You may, in this life, draw my queen
or my knave. My host, my domain, you must be brave.

Uncut Wood

Before the poem mars the page,
it speaks perfectly in the mind.
Before the children arrive,
they are unblemished and obedient.
Before the president takes office,
the people are hopeful.
When oils gleam their spirals
of burnt umber and crimson,
not yet brush-broken,
the canvas is flawless.

Crows snip worms, call: *Crave, crave, crave!*
One foot in childhood, one in the grave.
The Way endures forever,
a clean kitchen scarcely an hour.

Mortgage! Mortgage! scolds the Steller's jay
as I put the breakfast bowls away.
Blue song in the holly, sharp as joy, or theft,
flashes the crows on the wet roof.
It's easy to get lost along the way.

This morning, Plum Blossom Form
flowed through my hands
and from the net of heaven
rain fell on old snow.
The baby chewed his mysterious toes
content with a single tooth.

Lao Tzu, old carpenter, tell me the truth:
what's the difference
between *want for nothing*
and *good for nothing*?

What we love can always be taken.

The Ten Thousand Things

When your grandmother was alive
you were moving too fast to hear

her stories. When trees still stood, you wanted the mountain view
not uncut wood. Now you can't catch up

to her death. Her body's grit foamed like baking soda
as you flung her from the boat. The baby sat shiva, howled,

the sea threw salt in our eyes. Always
you thought there would be time

to learn and praise the ten thousand things.
You thought you could live without having to choose.

A woman's body is like a pot.
Where it's useful is where it's not.

You became the chambered nautilus,
prayer to thank God who had not

made you a man. Make space for wisdom, then,
child's palace growing in its bone moat,

heart above heart and all of the ten thousand songs
that lead to silence. Stand on one foot like a crane

hunting frogs in a ditch. Make wings of your arms.
Do nothing when the phone rings and someone calls to sell you

ten thousand things. Do you think you've accepted
the truth? Each life will go on until it stops

and you can't set the clock. You were just
the shock that got them started, their prehistoric myth.

Her blankets outlived her; they knit us together.
I wear her black wool coat in the rain.

We birth those who will scatter our ashes,
ten thousand pieces of bone.

What We Heard About Rain

How the rain
makes a shelter of wetness, how it gives birth

to the river, then rests.

—Alison Pick

She stopped her life to give birth
to the next generation

of words slipping out in a river
of blood, love of a man, good

or slipshod, unmoored love of a woman
for a woman. We know if we've chosen wisely

when the current takes us, when, crowning,
we split into upstream and downstream,

before and after, one and more
than one. Here is the mystery that never resolves—

something can be born out of nothing,
what was not can become: cloud and storm,

convergence of ether and desire,
chapped breasts, lanolin, broken-spined books.

We step into the same river,
changed. We camp under trees, dip

bare bottoms in clear water. Slippery, we hold them
on our laps as long as we can, watch rain drop

with a hiss into flame. We wash in the river, splash baby toes,
penises, rain on summer skin, soft as apricot

soft as the fingers of a lover on breasts
swollen with milk after a full day, first pushed away

in irritation, then allowed, as a river allows swans,
and our nipples harden into pits

as we allow ourselves to be carried away
by great need, as we allow life to pass through us,

to dirty our kitchens, hijack our thirties,
sweep us into its undertow

so we can't get our heads out. Feels like the goddamn rain
is a monsoon and we lose them in the supermarket

walk forty years in the desert, blind with tears, devastated,
before they pop out from behind the cucumbers

and we forget to buy milk, we forget who we are,
forget the way home. The rain doesn't let up and we can't sleep

pay bills get a job every five minutes the laundry buzzes
we're making lunch looking for the lost ballet slipper

the escaped frog the love we once felt that made us weak
in the knees, in bed, sore all over

abraded with love the rain won't quit and we can never
get it all done stretch marks appear on our hips

we are breathless, we wake up middle-aged,
like runoff on a river, channels of silver

in our hair, lines around our mouths.
From the moment they are born we succumb to nostalgia—

torrential thought—soon we'll be swept aside
we thought, we thought, we thought

what happened to us mattered, now we know
it's all and only them, we are never alone yet lonely,

fractured into refracting prisms, each life
that might have been, we are mothers

streaming ink in snow, riverbank undammed,
we give milk through the long night, quicksilver sheet,

the rain gives birth to the river.

Rain Song

I am the drummer of surfaces
the singer of all that's earth. Give me tin!

I'll thrill you, rat-tat-tatting your ears.
Give me stone, I'll sing hard music.

Give me time, and I'll erode you,
beat you softly with ten thousand fingers

until you surrender. Every day, I condense,
I bring wrath upon the peach blossoms, I monsoon

your villages, drown your cattle. I am the uninvited guest
at your shotgun wedding, I drench your white veil

tendril your upswept hair, I wash salt from the beach,
become the river. I am the rain, small tongues

fluted like snakes', I am the sound of peace
on flowering dogwood, spores

bursting underground, thrusting gold fingers
to meet my kisses, slick and silver. I am the snail's

companion, trail of drops illuminating the spider's web.
I am fresh tears of the gods

when they see what they have wrought.
I sing the song of cactus blooming after drought,

headlights sparkling into rainbow.
I am the fall and the resurrection,

the condensation, the evaporation. I am mist after great pain.
Ask me about erosion, how my mouth blunts mountains.

I am the rain.
I give birth to the river, then rest.

Maternal Sapphics I

I loved her body through the upheaval
of pregnancy. Loved her hot breasts
and the way she rose like fine wheat bread.
I loved that she never wore ugly maternity dresses
with green fish and bring-in-the-clown ruffles
as I once did, but stayed chic, androgyne
as she carried our son.

I loved watching her belly grow
like a man's beer gut. At night, while the big ones slept
in their tousled beds, I put my hand
over his aerials, her strong body
working overtime to carry more blood
to his need. O, good woman of my heart,
how still we lay in the truth of it:
soul and bones knit
sure as her hands on my face
in the throbbing dark.

Night polished the circlet of her beaten gold moon,
a wedding ring we did not care to own.

Maternal Sapphics II

As soon as she could walk, she checked herself out,
leaned on me past doctors who made her sign her own release
against their demands for more tests. We made it home.
Blue shadows grew under her eyes,
the sickness nursed on her,
we stopped speaking the same language.

My body was unmarred by his arrival.
Still, nothing was the same. The house, the family,
shifted to make room. In the garden, sunflowers hung
their red and yellow faces and I brought her bowls to vomit in,
broth she couldn't eat, books she couldn't read.
I wore him in a bundle on my chest
and hummed my way through the supermarket,
aisle after aisle of apples, my hand cupping his bruised head.
Strangers thought I looked remarkably unmarred
as mother to a newborn. I did not correct them.
There was too much to interpret.

Over the months her health returned,
summer's sun slipped into the ocean
like a placenta in a basin.
His father never knew that he'd been born.

Which is almost the same
as what we tell him, that he
doesn't have one, our double-mothered
love-tethered second son.

Maternal Sapphics III

I love him; how could I not? And her through him,
weary pilgrim to the body's holy lands.
I love the way the big ones love him,
pure goodness as they scrape his chin with flat spoons,
push the yams back in, grin when he pulls their faces close.

I do not love being left out here. No, I am not
supposed to say it, but sometimes I am the unwanted
unpaid babysitter, the rejected mother, the un-
biological. I'm sure I've grown spiritually
in a thousand ways that perhaps I'd rather not,
or maybe this is proof I haven't yet.
His sister explains what a father is,
A boy mommy, and you don't have one. No,
I don't want to be a dad, nor do I begrudge her
this sweetness I've twice known. But it's not mine.
Perhaps it's laziness on my part.
With no way to feed him, I have to work
to win his heart, but there are whole days
where nothing I offer makes any difference:
he wants her.

He wants her, and he has her. I will never be needed
to sing that song for him, song of milk and wholeness.
The days will make their own slow truths
as we learn our way toward each other.

Open the door's broken handle. Step outside.
Step out of language, out of tribe and custom.
Write my name in the book of ghosts.
What am I to him? I'm a different song,
song of longing, song
of not belonging.

Lullaby

Brave have I grown,
brave since you came.
When my death comes,
when dark grows my flame,
I won't protest,
I won't rage or fight,
I'll open my arms to the dying light—

As I opened for you, my firstborn son,
as my old self shattered,
and was reborn.
I'll meet death softly
in my white nightgown.
I'll meet death modestly, looking down.

How shall I leave?
How will I be gone?
The door slammed shut,
the house burned down?
A speeding truck, or cancer grown
into the ribs of my breast-empty gown?

I'll leave you bathed in salt
just as you arrived.
It will be your hand that shuts my eyes.
You'll be middle-aged and capable
on a boyhood street.
Someone else will hold you
as you meet your grief.

Coward have I grown,
coward since you came,
ambition abandoned,
hopes renamed.

If you must die,
let me die first.
This is my prayer:
Let me die first.
So you are blessed and so you are cursed.

Pinocchio

Joseph chiseled a child to answer to
his loneliness. On a cross of wood, a father
maneuvered strings, made his son dance
for our passion. The miracle was, he had no mother.
Of course there was a betrayal,
friends who shouldn't have been trusted. The vote
was rigged. But where did his conscience go? There it is, green
fiddler in the dark, hopping on the poppet's
shoulder. It wasn't only his nose that grew
with each lie. He had to die. Our sins demanded it.
But a resurrection's not impossible
at some point in this administration. The little dead
wooden limbs draped, pieta
in his virginal father's arms.
And on the morning of the last day, God said,
Let there be a whale to swallow you whole.
Let the innocent be punished
for their desires. Let the prayers of the father
create the living son.
The blue Madonna floated to midwife.
In the final stage of labour, Joseph wept.

What We Heard About Orphans

We heard there were millions of you,
each unique in your own particular tragedy,

in your third world villages, your American ghettos.
We wanted to take you home, give you all the good

we'd ever known. We heard you were our own
imperialism cloaked in motherhood.

That you might be sweet in babyhood, but we could
never know what you'd become. We heard

we were angels to take you in.
We heard you were stolen.

Orphan Song

We were told to hope for a new mommy and daddy,
and we hoped for a new mommy and daddy.

We were told we should be grateful to be chosen,
and we were grateful. There were chocolate kisses in your purse.

We heard our birth parents probably loved us very much.
Just not enough. We heard life was tough,

that we were lucky. We were taken out for dim sum, cherry blossom
festivals, lantern ceremonies, Ethiopian drumming.

There were shoulder rides, carousels. We beat our heels on your backs.
We heard whispers: our mothers had been whores,

had been raped, died of AIDS, had us too young. We put fingers
in our ears. We were wanted and not wanted.

Even before we could speak this new tongue,
we learned of love and impermanence,

and love, and impermanence.

What We Heard About Abortionists

You're shot at, bombs are planted
in your cars. You sweat in bullet-proof vests,

swear to tell the truth: the rate of abortion
is the same on either side of the law.

But without you, women die,
infected inside. You do your job,

preserve life. Certain contradictions
remain: a hundred million girls gone missing.

You do your job. O doctors of the elimination
dance, ministers of deliverance by un-

deliverance! Your job, which narrows down
to this row of women sedated, gowned

in blue, thighs juddering at the touch of your decisive
glove, as you make room, tug, ungestate them.

Perhaps they hold their husbands' hands,
perhaps not. The air is antiseptic, metal and blood.

Wool smothers their mouths, fug
of sour milk from chins they'll never wipe.

A thousand sleepless nights, worn-out shoes
have all come to this single cervical smart,

price of love or rape or lust:
unwelcome, uninvited guest, who, until

evicted, the room remade, blood quilt shed, plush
drapes drawn, has made them sick at heart.

Inside

Inside I hear my mother's heart.
I sit with my arms around my knees.

In my salt vat, I open and close my mouth.
I hold my cord when she trembles. It steadies me.

I'm anchored here. When she was knocked down
I was thrown inside her small sea. I am not

to be. A needle threads her arm.
She slept-with the wrong man.

A rock slips from the mouth of her womb.
She slept with the right man

at precisely the wrong time. She bruised him.
She was hurt long before I was a twinkle

in her eye. Which I am not. She has four children
and no one from church will ever know.

She has no room for a girl with a hole in her heart,
a thick tongue. I was going to die anyway.

I was perfectly healthy, but not according to tests.
I was unwanted, as is her constitutional right.

She couldn't sleep at night, trying to make up her mind.
She wanted me out. I never haunted her.

She wept to her sister in shame.
I was only lent to her. There is none other

to accompany me. In the dark
he touched his lips to her cheek.

Pennyroyal didn't do the trick.
A mind? Not yet. Only whispers.

Toes, yes, I have ten. Fingers translucent
as mushrooms in rain. They drift

like seaweed, trace my cheek.
I was dead before I could speak.

Spectacle & Feast

One morning we stepped into the garden
to gather dusty golden plums for breakfast.
The sun was already drawing resins
from blue-blossomed rosemary, slugs
were already curled around white
strawberries. The baby pointed out the rat
staggering under peach trees, matted, wet.
The cat strolled out, stage right,
flashed out a paw, slapped it flat.
With plum juice dripping on our bare feet,
with sweetness in our mouths,
we followed their pas de deux.
The rat tried to hide in a crack of rock
as the cat rolled on the stage of lawn
with all the time in the world
to play her part. She purred like a beehive.
She let the rat falter across the yard
before she strolled over,
languid as honey, pressed it into the rock,
chewed its naked tail a while. Then the rat
lifted its pointed, intelligent face,
touched its quivering nose to hers.
They smelled each other with great attention.
Whiskers trembling, the rat's face
moved over the cat's face
there on the boulder of morning. A hesitation,
a held, hopeful breath—but no, in the end,
of course not: the cat sprang to feast,
the rat screamed, the baby smashed
his hands together, clapping over my shoulder.
Nearby, a woodpecker clobbered its skull
on a pine: *encore, encore.*

Bat

She staggered round the playground in the sand.
Then hung from my sweater on hooked thumbs.
I let her cross from hand to open hand.
She licked her snout, licked salt from my palms.
I hid her in my jacket on the bus.
She was a black ball of yarn with two hooks.
She winked as if we had much to discuss.
I was nothing like those girls too scared to look.
The bat shimmied up my hair, grimaced a grin,
her face a puckered rose, drunk on sun.
Mother made me box the bat and drove us to town,
odd girl holding odd girl. They took her away, to be
undreamed by chloroform. Which I learned meant killed.
We screamed as our mothers held us down,
while the doctor stabbed and our fathers paid the bill.

Rabid fear quenched curiosity. Pain-trapped hands mapped flight.
But how many brats have been kissed by a bat?

Laureate

for Sam Green

From you I learned in order to be found
I must first find the words, the words with power.
How poems sleep like tulips underground
And then unfold in gratitude some hour.

But what of shame, that killing frost that burns
and blights the shy calypso of the valley?
And what of those who cannot find the words?
And what of narrow minds that turn away?

These old red barns that sing themselves to sleep
Here where the heron dips to catch its prey.
Here where the migrants pick our daffodils
and the Skagit River carries our poems away.

Wear your laurels lightly, my teacher
Poet of Waldron Island, wild Anacortes preacher.

Recipe for a Poem

Take something anyone can use:
how to set a broken bone, catch a net
of salmon, how to live alone
or how to live with someone a long time
without becoming lonely.

Add a hundred measures of reading late
into the still hours of the night.
Crawl back from hell on knees stained green
by sorrel. Open your mouth
and blow spore lighter than hope.
Add the scales of blind catfish,
stalactites from the underworld. An artichoke.

If the poet is out of patience,
add rue, a quarter cup chutzpah,
sprigs of curses, stems removed. Chop coarsely,
juxtapose with kosher salt and serve
at the temperature of a room
in which two people refuse to apologize.

If the poet is lost in a forest of symbols
beat in air vigorously until the whites
form stiff peaks. Toss in French, Greek,
break the line, snap meaning. Render fat.
Surrender hat. *Une faim de loup. Un cri du coeur.*
Marche comme un chat sur ses pattes.
Bake until meringue hollows, your mother's
midnight cries, peaks to tongue of stiff language glow.

O *jouissance.* If a silk moth lands on the poet's hand,
mix it in with a few quick strokes.
Catch the cries of love in damp sheets. Add sieved moonlight,
sifted twice. Benediction of cloth napkins.

If everything catches fire, beat flames with a fresh
manuscript. Douse in wine. Throw plates.

Guests should preferably be alive,
be able to walk a thin white line,
should remove their damp pairs of irony in the foyer,
drape their great woolen grief on the couch.
Let them come to the table with their mouths full of water,
onions in their pockets, hearts aching with the tongues
they knew by heart before they were born. Let them come.

What We Heard About the Mob

We surprise ourselves. An unknown talent
emerges. In a blink, we become collective. Smoldering

rage taproots down, ignites. Their accents revolt us.
The radio broadcasts suggestions. We are the swarm

of bodies, armpit tang, children on shoulders, cracked
teeth. Drag the body by a boot, hello, hello,

its arms flap over potholes. Don't trust
yourselves. Crush those who wear spectacles,

stack their skulls on shelves. We are peasants,
we are intellectuals, we play football.

The dog screams, pitch-forked to the wall.
The KKK burns crosses in moonlight.

We were breastfed, we were cradled,
we were kissed and beaten.

Chairs shiver through glass,
our grins reflect silver. We liberate a candelabra,

leave a footprint in blood. Three cut knuckles.
We are original, we are pure,

we discover the other use for fire.

What the Mob Perhaps Heard

Die, said a man
with a machete to another man

with a machete, and we ran like boys
or perhaps we ran like lions. *Kill,* said the officer

and we broke down the door to dig out the dogs
who hid in the attic

until we shot overhead
and blood screamed through

the holes in the floor. Catholic. Jew.
Serbian. Hutu. There was a girl who fed stray

cats. We all wanted to fuck her,
she sat at the knee of the midwife,

night into morning and caught babies.
The fat on her bones popped

in our flames. There were Armenian men
singing in the street in Istanbul,

and then there weren't.
A Jewish cantor lifted his voice.

A nun said *Je vous en prie,* she took a bullet in the throat,
she opened her eyes. There were cowboys on Indian ponies

who went hunting Indians, and the sound
they heard was their own hearts, pounding.

Heard *This is a good day to die.* This is a good day
to belong. There was a marching band.

We were following orders. We were sleepwalking.
It was too hot. We had to do it or be killed ourselves.

Some other time, we would have poured you tea,
given you our own beds with hand-sewn quilts.

We didn't start it.
We can't look at our hands when it's over.

But then the bodies are buried.
We move into their empty houses.

Rain clears the blood fug,
peach trees blossom.

Like babies we learn to sleep through the night,
to self-soothe. Gradually our hair turns silver.

Fags Die, God Laughs

—protest sign

1.

She laughs a volcano
from heels to massive belly. She laughs
earthquakes. Tremors from her breasts
cause floods in several mid-western states. She laughs
an avalanche that spills over the Sierra Nevada
mountains. She roars with laughter
through Christian Arkansas, smashes a thousand
innocent heterosexual trailer homes.
She laughs an oil spill, invaginates
the Gulf Coast in lightweight crude, punishes the atheist
pelicans. She laughs and floods Pakistan, folds
Sri Lanka in tsunami to say Ha, ha,
too bad you chose the wrong god! She washes away
whole villages as the women go out at low tide
to gather fish. She dangles broken bodies
in the flood-torn trees of Burma like temple baubles
because it tickles her. You dare to believe you know her mind,
she who cannot be contained?

2.

And who are we to think we can distinguish his laughing
from his crying?

3.

There would have been a brother among brothers, different and the same,
but there was not.
There would have been an opportunity, a conversation,
but there was not.
There would have been a door and a song,
but there was not.

There would have been a barbed wire fence empty of flowers,
but there was not.
There would have been a museum of secrets, baskets of bread and chocolate,
but there was not.
There would have been a prophet of desire, a swarm of fritillaries,
but there was not.
There would have been the sanctity of breath in the body,
but there was hate.

What We Heard About the Americans

We heard there was much to admire about the Americans.
Historically.

Their cuisine is buffet, all you can
overeat.

We heard they hire whisperers, buy guides for
idiots.

Foster special needs kittens. Are visited by
aliens.

We heard the Americans are our
brethren.

That they keep ten percent of black men
imprisoned.

Are stockpiling weapons for
Armageddon.

Believe that all good dogs go to
heaven.

God bless the Americans. God bless their inalienable
freedoms.

Bless Guantanamo. Americans sure know how to have
fun.

Even their deaths are more important than our
own.

Happiness is cosmetic
dentistry.

The global dream is the American
dream.

Liberty is a statue holding a soft ice
cream.

What We Heard About the Canadians

We heard they were not American.
Not British and not quite French.

They were not born in Hong Kong
did not emigrate from Russia with a single pair of shoes.

They were not all russet-haired orphans
who greeted the apple blossom dawn with open arms,

crying *Avonlea!* They were not immodest,
did not want God to save the Queen.

Their leaders were not corrupt.
They were not all Mounties on proud horseback

with hot tasers. *Fuck me* was not considered impolite
in their living rooms.

There was no great Canadian hush of things not to be talked about.
Not all of them ignored genocide.

Not all of them sang a "cold
and broken Hallelujah" as the bells broke crystal ice

across parc Lafontaine. They were not rich and also
not poor. Not overachievers. Neither believers nor unbelievers.

C'etait pas toute l'histoire, and they would not
be caught clubbing seals on TV, red bloom

on white coat, melting eyes. They did not mine asbestos
in Quebec, make love in skidoos,

sleep in snowshoes. Never danced hatless
under dancing Northern lights. They were polite.

Hymn to Shit: Four Movements

1.

Morning sit on white throne
perched above tea-stained bowl

     sound of water!

2.

Shit, I sing your hymn of fullness.
I praise the feast, so must I praise
hunger's dark offspring.

Shit, you are the swamp's sweet-sick
daughter, you are the trough's brown son,
gut's coiled casings,

                 artifact of banquet.

To squat or to sit, that is the question.

          O asscheeks' bullseye!
          O sisterhood of shitters!

    Let us go then, I and you,
    To the outhouse strung with cobwebs hung with dew.
    Oh, do not ask, "How clean is it?"
    Let us go and make our visit.

3.

O chamber pot of my island girlhood,
O mother's chore of boiled diapers,
chapped hands, cedar outhouse my father built,
the words he carved around the seat
my childhood mantra:

Pooh Here.

O island cougar, pacing the back pasture.
Terror of night's path to the outhouse.
Solo roll of toilet paper softening
in its tin can, sowbugs dropping down,

                        down

      Fetid spectacle! Flies serenade
           August outhouse hole.
                 O soft brown star-nosed mole,
                     full moon
          rumpus.

4.

Toilet paper is pink in Paris
white in Vancouver. Better
bring your own to Shibuya Station!
Use salal leaves on Salt Spring Island. From this end
we're all in it together.

     *   *   *

Have you loved someone enough in this world
that they will change your sheets, change
your diapers, lift your cold feet in their supple hands
and rub in the fragrant oil?

There is still time.
You are not dead yet.
Go, love someone that much.

Ablution

In the beginning was darkness—

Puffins sun themselves on outcrops of rock
snug seniors in beach chairs. Aleutian Babylon of cliffs,
they fight with cormorants for the best spot, chat
around two or three flat silver fish

garnishing their bright beaks, each tipped
with orange arrowheads that dip
toward the place where moon slipped
beneath ocean

some hours before. In sorrow
sun palls its light in mist,
wet shawl cast over a lamp.
We are too far gone for trees.

After long darkness upon the face of the deep,
let there be light. Let there be multitudes of birds
in the firmament above.

Two dozen men have been shipped in to reopen the gold mines.
There are two trucks and one dirt road. I mind
my small brother, help the cook mop grit
from the floor three times a day, drown

my grey mop-head in greasy water, erase
tracks of miners' boots, their jokes, their hunger.
Ablution. At night we sleep with our faces
to the sun, thin curtain half unstrung, saturated with light.

We drink when we thirst, lie down
when we're tired and sleep in full sun.
We stick our arms in among salmon
pirouetting upriver to spawn. We grow numb

catching them, thick-lipped Kings
longer than my brother. Neat as bears
we throw them to shore, flip tail over head,
drag them back in buckets for the cook to prepare.

In the firmament below,
let there be salmon! When ye eat thereof
let the flesh fall apart as the petals of a rose.

When a miner developed a taste for me,
I did not know why. His hands are now
inseparable from that landscape. Once I ran with my brother
through bogs of white orchids I couldn't trust,

our tracks revealed in stinking plants
that bruised and bled black under our boots.
I dreamed I would sneak away, alone
after the light had gone, when all the mines were blocked

and the men had flown home. I wanted to watch the ermine
lose their summer brown, white against snow,
their endless game of freeze-tag past midnight.
I wanted to be here by myself

tagged, already frozen, unobserved,
breathing with volcanoes, white mist
into moist light, cloud torn to an illusion of moon.
Once I walked into miners' cabins, built a century ago,

slowly settling back into the landscape.
Doors without locks, windows holding glass
thick at the base, as a woman's ankles
thicken with age. Detritus

of wasps and flies, blue
milk of magnesia bottles cracked on the floor,

a perfect wooden rocker that rocked on its own
when the wind knocked.

I hid with my brother, breathing in the hot dust
until my father called us home. On the shore
an ancient forest had turned to stone.
Petrified. I cared and I didn't care.

I washed and washed myself, rebraided my hair.
I said nothing to anyone about his hands
or my body, the landscape drenched in light,
summer-brown ermine that shape-shifted

through deserted mine shafts, stalactite,
water becoming dripstone, me becoming, he said,
a woman, geodes cracked in back of the truck, my body,
his hands, the unanswered prayers, the light.

A Mystery

Not what was done to you, girl,
but how you survived it,
that's the great mystery. Not survived
like a cow survives the taking of her calf,
all brown-eyed pain and damage,
but like the quail that drags her wing,
pretending it is broken
to lure the coyote away from her small selves.
Where did you, each of you, find such strength?
That you could know it was not in you,
the shame, it was not of you, not yours, and you didn't have
to bear it. Love had gotten to you first.
Someone who adored you had sung you to sleep,
brushed the tangles from your hair, inoculated you.
Someone gave you the right books before you knew
you needed them. Someone else took you to the mountains
and showed you with his own two hands
how to make fire, build temporary shelter.
Of course you carried it somewhere,
we know that, like a handkerchief stiff with blood.
Sometimes it fell over your face, a veil to keep out the light,
sometimes you stuffed its rot in your mouth and howled.
But it didn't become you. You let touch pleasure,
you became yourself. I commend your mysterious courage.
You let what happened once
become a legend, a long time ago.
Sometimes at night you rock it in your arms, singing, *Hush,
hush memory,* like a mother empty of self, then lower it
to its broken cradle, shut the door.
You might tell your children
when they are grown,
but only if they need to know,
only if the moon is full
and the crow's shadow falls in your mouth.

Daphne to Peneus

When Apollo taunted Eros, I was handy
for revenge. I was lovely then—
reason enough to draw wrath. Apollo stalked me
in the market, his fantasy
blinding the indifferent crowd. They thought
he was my boyfriend. Or a god. I believed
you'd save me, Father, but not like that.
I called for you as he caught me and cleaved
his way in. Under him I turned to wood.
He peeled back my indifferent bark,
buried himself in dry mosses. Could
you hear my bones snap, feel my bloodsap
in your river? I grew where you said I should.
Years drift, friends become legends, I'm still wood.

Aubade: Grendel's Mother

You left sick-scent on the sheet, Geat.
Damn your thigh salamander
and my weakness for armed men.
You pledged a solemn sword, mer-mate,
spelunked my pits, slippered
into my nights, heart-hassled me. Now
you turn from swamp-stink, from paternity, boast
of defeating demon-daring darkness. Once
I begged of you: Oath me, oath me!
How I loved you then: fool-femme
wanted a boast-bastard.

Say merewif. Say Lady Green-hair.
Take my dare, blood-drunk Christ-worshipper.
Enter my lake-lair. Lie with me a little, Beowulf.
O son-killer, monster-fucker,
once we tussled like siblings, we wrestled, brother—
you tasted my mouth sweeter than sex-slime
before the cross came between us.

Now you are afraid the world will see
Grendel has your blue eyes. He strays to your throne
night after night, howls for his father.
My enemy, it is meet that we meet
in the mead-hall where you ripped off his arm,
bled the boy dry. Fie!

I come for your life. This is the weregild price, cost of a son.
Bearskin-wearer, grave-digger, you twisted
plaits that once shone gold, you called
my breath foul, my skin scaled, defamed my beauty,
named me fiend-form, bent back my neck with iron,
cleaved until the soul sank. Breast-broken,
sword-stabbed, I fled to peat and bog.
Unmothered. Deity of the dead.

But you did not kill me, King. Damned, I am
reborn. Fire-tongued dragon-dame, I'll yet come
home. Goddess of the chthonic swamp—
church-defiled, witch-suckled—I'll take my slow revenge. Liege,
I will lie no longer under your poem. I'm poison.
I spit flame on you and the dawn-dogs flayed
to escort your death-ship boat-trip
to the underworld, Dane. You're going down.

Aubade: Buddha's Wife

Others worship you, but I loved you, husband.
I still think we could have worked it out.
You named our newborn son Rahula, *Fetter*,
and fell into post-partum despair at his birth. Did your father
bind you to such grief when he kept old people a secret
all your boyhood, forced the broken-bodied outside city walls,
grandparents banished? Or was it your queen mother, who died
and left you? Life is a nut meat in our mouths, and life
is a bowl of cobwebs too. Once
Queen Maya sat under the ashoka trees
and held their red flowers to her face, heavy with joy,
tracing the *linea nigra*, as inside her you dreamed
of great loneliness, and beat your heels against it. Seven days
after your birth she died, her right side still clotted with blood.
You drank the milk of a woman your father paid,
who felt the death of her own child in every pull.
You grew fat on her sorrow; it formed your dimples.
I can't forgive you. For how many lifetimes will my heart
be shackled to yours?

We suffer, we die. Are you to be honoured
for discovering this, as if you'd found a new country?
You left us with a kiss while we were sleeping.
The rosy dawn was terrible to me. O my vagabond,
should I have followed your example, left our son to drift
unfettered, without even my milk to nourish him?
Did you feel lighter as you wandered,
eating fallen mangoes, sitting with stray dogs
who pushed their noses in your palm
for salt? Whole philosophies of attachment
unbind the breasts of ordinary mothers
who will never do what you've done.
Idiot. He never knew your hands.
Yes, we will die, yes, there is pain.
You could have stayed home, Siddhartha.
You could have raised our son.

Song for the Unbeliever Who Wishes to Believe

Pity me. I do not have it in me
to wear the crown of thorns. I won't carry the cross
of love for the world. I can't be Buddha—desire in my bed
tickles my ribs like a knife. I don't know Kannon,
goddess of mercy—I have two arms for the world's endless
pain. Mother Kali, with her pockets
of two-headed coins, does not know my name.
My feet stumble, I'm afraid
to follow Shiva's dance. I cannot be Aisha,
Muhammad's bride at nine, though I too
have turned back to search long for a lost necklace.

But I can be like Mary, a little. Once I was pregnant
with mystery. Revelations unfolded in me,
a mouth yawned in my dark waters.
I chose the unseen spirit.

As a girl I slept in a barn, beside a girl
I no longer know. We were both virgins then.
Already her faith had manifested
into a hard gold cross between her full breasts;
already I lacked both cross and cleavage. Mice skittered
in the grain bins. An owl flew in
and we flew out, screaming through the dark pasture,
no more aware than Aisha
of the courses our girlhoods would take, split
like the stream that ran through the woods between our houses,
drawing sap from hallowed maples. Church lightning.

Silver. And weren't you Persephone once,
drawn to the god of fire, temple of smoke,
and didn't your mother save you?
And weren't you Lot's wife,
deadened with the weight of exile?

Once you knew the language of belief. You were empty
as a baby in a basket worn out from crying
at the moment someone who would love you as her own
sang down the path, unbinding her hair.

Shamhat to Enkidu

Enkidu, come in from the desert.
Leave your scavenging
and crawl to my knees,
part my civilized rose. Cup
wet musk. Bring me your face.
You smell like a ram. I taste like cedar in the rain.

Look: I have fire, I have sex.

Wrestle me by the deep wells
for seven days and nights. I will tame you,
wild man, I'll drop fermented honey
into your mouth. Look: I have vocabulary.
My hair is hung with bells.
I have a silver knife and bowl.

I'll lead you to the man
who will be your best friend,
who will teach you the love of battle,
a power greater than my own.
You will forsake me for him
and then the word for what I am will be lost:
Harlot-Priestess, the one who knows the source.

Centuries later my only followers
will be forced to the profession:
Stolen girls, who grease their breasts
and dance around poles to tame men for money.
Bodies of my priestesses will be dumped
in alleys, stuffed in the trunks of cars,
left to bloat in rain. Men will thumb bills, cock
needles. There will be no worship in the act.

Enkidu, I should have left you with the beasts.

I was your touchstone, your red dust whore.
I gave you words so Gilgamesh could give you war.

Cock Song

All you do is call attention to yourself,
stir up trouble. You're a bit thick, yes.

Your fans are the banana, the cigar,
the slide trombone.

Is that a gun in your pocket?
Your Cyclops eye weeps golden tears.

You are a velvet-cloaked night-bandit,
lone diminutive of presidents named Richard.

You are a spotted pudding we'd rather not fork. You drool.
Your vocabulary is puny.

You think *bullseye,* you think *score.* Heat
makes you cocksure and rosy, cold clenches you like a worm.

You insinuate yourself into conversations,
glory holes, brief slits. You rise with the sun.

Your cap is doffed by doctors and rabbis.
Fragrant and faithless, seedful.

Red-faced chap, why rib your raincoats? You can't fib
your need. Wax fat, wane thin. Wipe your chin.

Rose Song

Don't cry wolf. Just call it a *moule*,
a Gertrude, an oyster, a wound, a matrix

an orchid, an anemone, a box, shame,
slash, crack, bud, gash, clam.

Don't cry wolf. Rose is a rose is held down,
blood working to clot, severed,

ghosts of gasped desire,
bursts against a lover stillborn to scar.

If a rose blooms in the forest where no one sees it.
If a rose blooms and is devastated. If a woman scrapes with a blade

and remembers how it was done to her.
If a child walks with great difficulty. If a woman repents.

If a man and a woman make love in a ditch.
If a bath is clogged with petals. If he knocks you down

and brings you roses.
If the petals stain.

If the memory stains.
If we could return to the garden.

Tired

Sucede que me canso de ser hombre
It happens that I am tired of being a man
          —PABLO NERUDA, "WALKING AROUND"

It happens that you are tired of being a man,
Poet, and I am tired of men.

You're tired of barbershops,
they make you weep, and I am tired of men

whose oil leaks slick the sea and can't be capped.
You're tired of being a man

who describes the blood of children in the streets.
You're tired of love, old man.

What is the name for a man with a poon?
If I were a glass of wine, and you a different kind of man,

together we could taste oblivion, we could spit on the moon.
If I happened, dear man,

to call you back from the dead, a wrong number on the line,
and you said you no longer required the shape of a man

but preferred the bees' wax rooms
or the resin of an ancient pine, we'd be free of human

form. I'm tired of difference.
I'm tired of being a woman.

The newspapers are inked in misery,
bombs are wired to handsome men—

why, Rachel, have you let verse drag you down again,
fallen in love with a woman who thinks like a man?

The Opposite of War

The opposite of war takes half an afternoon
costs seven dollars in parking
and does not solve the problem
we cannot solve. It is inconvenient
and stings a little.

It does only what it says it can do:
gives blood to strangers for a little more life,
a little more life. The opposite of war
has its arm on a table
with a tourniquet around it.
It goes on and on.
It looks away
from thoughts of the man
who becomes a bomb.

The opposite of war comes down
to how the word *stranger*
is translated:
one blood sacrifice
or another.

Cherry trees create a spectacle, tossing their wet confetti
at the window. A child's hair falls out
on her pillow. Blood pools under the skin
of the sky. We're dizzy now. Our blue gift
flashes red at the exit. We don't speak to each other,
but we're lighter when we leave.
The opposite of war is not useless,
but nearly so. It bruises.
We get a cotton ball to staunch the flow.

Drone

For Karim Alrawi

Glaze eyes. Then glaze soul: the dull, dull deadly
dull faceless work of those killed
whose names we don't know
by those whose names we don't know. Drone:
we can't mourn or condemn
because we can't see. It's a hive of bees,
it just stupefies us, we breathe in the smoke
smoke, smokescreen war, collateral damage, compound
fracture. Smart bombs kill only bad men
and those who chose the wrong side: suspect wives,
bodyguards, accidental children,
a cat on a wall of stone. Drone. In a hotel room,
eyes half-mast, he sucks the plastic spout of a honey bear,
drifts to the place where poppies come from.
It doesn't help if we shout: he's gone. Gone.

It doesn't count if you do it standing up. If you do it
with good intelligence. If you do it from very far away
so they are small ants so they don't know
what hit them. What hit them? Lemons
hail at impact. They want to minimize
casualties, improve accuracy.
We are too far away to hear the news,
we hang upside down, there are Djinn of dust,
we swarm the enclave, clean the stingers,
strum our throbbing abdomens,
swell our lethal hexagons. Drone.

It's good hygiene. No broken bodies
on screen, just the buzz of America's Biggest
Loser, just the long, long boring war.
So turn the channel already, bury first-born souvenirs
sent home on ice, medicate all post-coital

stress syndrome. Drone. When there's no spectacle,
how can we mourn? One button,
and they are erased: a slight tornado
of dust, unwrapped chest, fractured
human shield. Her arms relax, she spills
her body's wine: blood
dervish, tea and teaspoon.
Eyelashes: son. Drone.

Drunk

You take your son and daughter to the lake
to feed the ducks—you hold your daughter's hand
and run, flapping through the small daisies, then fall down,
kicking your legs in sync with her legs,
laughing. Your son watches from a bench, calls,
"Mama, are you drunk *again*?" The couple
bike-riding past look over their shoulders,
an old man raises his binoculars.
It is the *again* that gets you, as though
every day you get drunk and drag your children
out to chase mallards. As though he's ever seen you
drunk, your carefully protected firstborn,
as though you manage to drink more than a glass
of red a couple times a month. You tell him
that he will *never* see you drunk,
and something in your voice stops you both
from saying more. You give them their bread crumbs
and watch as through a glass, darkly,
their delight at the painted turtles who poke shy beaks
up from under the ducks. You swallow the tannic memories,
protective of them: they will not know what it is
to see Grandma passed out on the upstairs bed, to see Grandpa
raving with alcohol, prophet in a cave, flinging his dark
sticky curses on her vacant face. Your son will not,
as you did, hold your mother's hand and lead her
crying from their house back to her car, and he will also not
be grateful for this, though it has cost,
because he will not know.
Just as a woman you love recalls
with wonder her son saying,
after she told him to clean up the flour he'd spilt,
"Mama, was anyone ever as mean to you as you are to me?"
and how she swallowed her words, remembering her father
who whipped her shoulders with metal hangers,
and *No*, you didn't understand your father's rage, but you knew

the taste of fear, though he would say he protected you all his life
from the wooden spoons his mother used
to beat the questions out of him. No.
They will not understand what they have been spared
because we have also spared them this
knowledge. We have swallowed it and set our lips,
knocked back that ancient vintage,
those complicated, full-bodied, stone fruit notes
that linger on the finish.

5 a.m. winter run in fog

They say one day we will miss the noise
when we are alone together in our quiet house.
Today I miss silence. I get up at five
and go running after it, through huge trees
hung with mist, dark branches
against smudged sky. Which flour print
on the black apron of night
is the moon, working to cast its light
through fog?

My days are like that,
noticed when I'm eclipsed,
when I don't do my job, don't unclog,
don't wipe, don't get us there on time.
How they rush me when I open the door,
grab me around the knees
in their passion, which I, like any imagined deity,
did nothing to deserve, which they created
out of need for something to worship.

The baby is quiet's opposite. He is shrieking now,
in his fat diaper, wearing his sister's pink boots
that reach his thighs. He touches my hair as I return,
wet with drops of mist. He yells,
searching for language, as I search for silence,
something I misplaced with the mates of socks,
cars without wheels, lost marbles.

Don't tell me what love is:
I can never not, now.

Love-briars work their way under my skin,
ingrown, an infection
of worry, ache of their new teeth,
the way they pat my bumped hip and kick

the bad door that smacked me, yes,
the way they pronounce *stegosaurus*.

In his stroller, the baby smiles in his sleep,
old tears standing on his cheeks.
His sister follows me around with her violin, scaling
Oh, Come Little Children. His brother
wants to tell me a joke about two boys
who happen to be named
Poop and *Shut Up*.

Maybe the baby will have a good nap,
we'll all pick up a library book on trains, read together
with their bodies on my body
until softness enters my arms again.

Will I find them again,
those carefully measured days,
like I find those socks, cast off and stuck with mint
in the cushions of the couch? Will I call them
good as new or will it be too late,
will they no longer fit?

What We Heard About the Universe

We heard it was infinite, beyond
the beyond of the song of songs

and we tried to picture it, but it hurt.
Einstein said *Imagination is more important*

than knowledge. We consoled ourselves with this,
pressed our eyes with fists and made gold blots ringed in violet.

We heard the universe was finite, folded
upon itself, akin to an accordion,

cosmic cunt, capable of infinite expansion
when a new light was born.

We heard it contained its own death,
our world, all worlds. Black holes

loomed to consume; there could be no God,
just the void we would become.

We heard we might collide
with another sun. Of course we were anxious:

from the bottom of a well, even when the sun shines,
we could see stars. We're alone with each other.

Perhaps we broke up due to differences
in density. Nobody answers our RSVP.

Don't talk to me of chaos. A long time ago, energy was borrowed
recklessly. The universe is in more debt than the U.S.

What a cosmic hedge fund! We'll die. It could be worse.
The night filled your eyes with stars.

In some parallel universe, you never left.
The moon shone among the orange persimmons

as we huddled in your coat. Stars were thick as semen
in a Petri dish, and we pressed together, drenched

as the milky way. Yearning is the universal condition.
You have your own dark energy to worry about.

Shalom. Namaste. Another dawn will come.
Palomino-pulled chariot, bridal gown undone.

What the Universe Perhaps Heard

Beluga banter, tongue of stars
white noise: wonder what we are.

No atmosphere, clouds undone,
the fire-pop plasma of newborn suns.

Silent vacuum, blush of snow
hush now, thrum light undertow.

Delivery Room Under Renovation

for Susan, for Alec Michael

The night my water broke, a week early,
I held my wide sides and rocked, knowing
that before another day came, no matter what the pain,
she would be born. And then I went upstairs
to my quiet study. It was two a.m. and my last chance
to be alone with poetry for what I knew,
the second time around, would be a long
exhausted, milk-pocked haul. Every time I stood
to take a book down from the shelf, waters
poured out of me. I sat and wrote until the contractions
became too strong. Slowly I was drawn by the rope
around my hips, dipped in and out of that well
of pain. In between I sipped rose tea,
marked a few last-minute changes on a manuscript,
dripped and dripped and dripped.

In the hospital a day later, they handed me a baby
in the recovery room. My abdomen had been
stapled shut. I was numb from the ribcage
down. We were in a room full of the knock and rattle
of jackhammers. Plastic sheeting covered the drywall remodel.
"You should breastfeed her now," said the nurse,
and I couldn't quite believe it. "*Now?*" I complained,
more child than mother, "I'm pretty tired right now,"
but the nurse set her lips, untied my hospital gown,
helped that tiny rosemouth yawn and latch
onto the breast. I gasped as the baby's tugs burned
thin skin, then laughed at her fine round face
as she squinted at us, blinking her eyes,
and we were blessed, and wiped our eyes.

The nurse, leaning over my bed, said to us
they were bringing a woman to recovery
whose baby had just died. She did not need

to ask us to stifle our delight. The woman was wheeled in,
moaning but sedated. The nurse pulled the curtain
around her bed, and I held my newborn, her eyes
still glistening with erythromycin, small white bonnet
pulled over her wet hair, and only a thin curtain
separated me from the mother whose baby had died:
I don't mean a metaphorical curtain. I mean a thin
green hospital curtain on a metal track.
I wished to, but dared not, pull it back.

I Might Be Nothing (Lara's Song)

Now you are not
part of the visible world, now you are nothing
but recollections, dim as a dust-stricken room
in Chinatown, where I lived on Princess
and wanted to be one
and you lived with your mother
who made art and loved you
and we played on the floor and that is not
nothing.

You might have been anything. You got caught
in something too fraught to untangle.

           You might have been
seen in an alley, picked up by a stranger in a Jaguar.
You might have been washed gently in the hospital
where you were born. You might have been reborn. An ordinary
mother of two. Famous. A doctor. Safe.

Your mother comes to meet my children.
She gives them your frog puppet
because she has no use for it any more.
She says, "Tell me if I'm talking too much.
I love to talk about her."

If I could get a fix off blame, beveled
like a needle in a vein, I'd do it. Smoke my spoon, my heart.

The puppet disappears in our basket of toys.

Later when my daughter finds it,
I snatch it, say, "That's not a toy!" But what
is it? An artifact.
I hand it back.

What We Heard About the Sea

Once we belonged. We belonged for wet
millenniums. We exiled ourselves

gill by gill. The sea sang us forth,
first birth, first Eden,

our blood tide brackish. The Fall
was a struggle to shore, sip of sharp air.

We can't even name how we long to go home,
but still that desire

swims in us. We return to visit
with buoyancy compensators, masks

and tanks of air, we sink, remember
how it felt to live here,

but we are tourists now. Cold gold
light in water, we touch brittle fingers

of black coral, feathered tongues of barnacles,
even the great wings of manta rays

soar over us. We suck hungrily
on our mouthpieces, swallowing back our salt,

yearning for the time when we lived here,
when we could fly.

What the Sea Perhaps Heard

Killer whales hunt a blue whale calf
and eat his tongue. As he bleeds to death,

blood seeps without a sound into my body.
Gulls come, screaming their belly-greed,

small fish unstitch flesh with needle teeth.
The mother blue has more grief

In her massive body
than anything else I have held.

No one has seen what I see: how great white
sharks copulate, fitting together in secret method.

When the octopus siphons me inside her,
and I unfurl her delicate legs with warm currents,

she blushes for me alone. I hold the tight curl
of the seahorse's tail as he pivots,

protecting his basketful of life.
Observe the spaghettini arms of starfish

reaching for drifting food. Hear their little song:
the stomach, the stomach! Dear urchins, sweet limpets,

all feast in me. In the heat of my armpit
waves curl their black seaweed, stones groan

as they are ground to sand. I rock them.
In my cold brain I am rational,

I do not weep to feel the polar bears
scrape my frozen cheeks.

I do not weep when belugas
sing or narwhales leap like unicorns

and when icebergs collapse I am
scraping dead skin from my forehead

so I can think better: that thunderous, cleansing
crash. Sometimes I catch your broken boats

and your broken bodies, your diamond necklaces,
your New World apple trees. I accept everything,

I turn no one away. That's me gripping your line, your net,
your boots in invitation, dragging your thighs as you run.

At dawn the grey whale fills his baleen
with a noise like water falling through feathers

and at dusk you sail your boats
across my belly, dragging your hands

as you stare into the wet green silk, as a child peers
under his mother's dress

thinking she won't notice, to see
where he came from.

Delilah

for Jen and Gabriela

You turned two women into mothers, transformed them entirely,
reshaped them with the hard tools of love and grief
into women stronger than they had any right to be.
You changed the world! Brief spark burning,
you flared and illuminated for many
what it means to be human and vulnerable,
what it means to be open to birth and death.

Their arms will ache with your absence,
they will be heartsick without you.
They spent every moment they were given loving you.
They will remember your weight, your perfect shape
in their arms, how they learned to love each other
through the worst nights, how they held on to one another,
did not let go,

even when you let go.

The night your spirit left your body,
they carried you outside
into the garden, into the dark and beautiful
garden. Their arms trembled
knowing you were gone. The night trembled
with birdsong.

But look: all over the world, we still see you!
Just today in my garden, a golden butterfly rose
to brush the lilacs. At dusk in California, a hummingbird,
ruby throat pulsing, opened a sunflower
and drank like a small prayer of courage, courage!

You opened us to love
as the sun opens roses to its great shining.

—May 1, 2005

The Argument

The argument went on all spring,
me versus my despairing student.
Once in the hall, I turned from her
wet eyes, disgusted
with us both.

Once I was sure I'd reached her.
Listen, I said, *listen:*
when a poem gives up its liquor,
when the grey-eyed baby on the bus waves at you,
when your murdered brother
runs through the apple orchard
of your dreams, tell me
you don't feel it then, the gift of your own
breath?

She listened politely. I spoke
another language. Her tongue
was sorrow. I tried to reach her
through the receiver
as light left the sky, as the children
stole candy from the cupboard,
tumbling over each other—
in truth I longed to hang up.

People love you, I argued, not knowing
if what I said were true. She sobbed through the phone.
Once I put her down to stir the onions.

She entered the hospital, left against orders. I called.
I missed her call. We all broke
confidence for the good of her health. I left
the country, left her in professional hands. She had pills,
a plan, a support team.

She needed a brother
to batter her demons with boxing gloves.
She needed a mother to eat her tears.

You never know what mystery awaits you,
I told her once. *Count on it.* Though my words
weighed less than the air on her skin.
Joy will find you again, I said, as if speech
could make it so. I made her promise to call
before she harmed herself.

When news of her death flew across the Pacific,
I sat in a temple on Mount Koya, eyes dry
as rock. My children watched me light incense.
A clear-faced nun helped me strike the bell
and prayers rose in smoke's choke.

They say a wolf, caught in a trap,
 will bite through its own leg
to escape. Sometimes a woman
will leap from her own balcony
to set herself free.

Spectacle

It was déjà vu, the grief tableau,
to drive back to that cemetery today
the one that takes the dead who pay
and the dead who cannot pay.

Last spring I dressed for another suicide,
a refugee, married at thirteen,
who left orphans behind,
who bartered her life for oblivion's bargain.

They had to rent two school buses
to get all the mourners to her grave,
The children sang the songs from Burma,
songs of good-bye. Women said they were sorry
they hadn't helped her more.
A man said he was sorry
men hadn't loved her better.
When the earth fell from our communal shovel
and it was all over, a small girl
slipped her hand into mine.

You got none of that. We stood, five
around your grave down the slope
from where another woman's body deliquesced
in its satin box. I wore the same blouse. We waited
in hot sun for the Imam.
Each car that passed we hoped was his,
but yours was a suicide, and no one
came. Staff told us to begin, but we were speechless,
unprepared, when the moment came.

I was the teacher who taught you nothing. I read
a poem. An honest man recalled your pain,
clear-faced women poured dirt
with their own hands. That was all.

I did not make a spectacle of myself until
they put the marker on your grave
with your name spelled wrong,
would not fix their mistake
without the proper paperwork,
which might take a week or might never come.

The backhoe tucked you in.

I am done with that place, I swear it,
but you are not done with me.
Trying to sleep, I felt wind rushing past
your freefall. I startled awake, gripped
the sides of the bed, wrote you
this last poem.

Once you read to us in Farsi.
You wore your glasses on a silver chain. Today
the sun burned its calculations into the manicured lawn.
At your grave, white carnations
scattered in fresh earth
like shattered teeth.

What We Heard About the Suicide

We heard it wasn't our fault.
We heard you left a note,

scrawled when poison
stole your voice. We heard you left no reason.

You were alone. You borrowed a gun.
We heard you didn't mean to swerve.

Everywhere you went, bridges called you.
Cliffs made the soles of your feet ache.

From a hundred living rooms,
we watched your slow death on the internet.

When you left, the same rain
still blurred our windows. Pollen drifted over the freeway

near your apartment as we dragged away your blood-thick bed
before your parents came. Your smell fogged our hair.

The first time you shot into your own
supple vein, you knew your name

was an anagram of gone.
We heard the radio play what was once your song.

What the Suicide Can't Hear

The window's shut, the phone cord cut.
The world outside is muzzled. You are in your bedroom

hating your hands, hating your mother's thin wrists
and your father's tendency toward despair

made manifest in you. What we love too much,
what we grip in fear, you abandon. If

you could hear that everything changes,
even this, would you stay? If

you opened your window on the world
of the Lord in whom you don't believe,

what would you hear? Blast
of leaf blower, distant siren,

a mother yelling *Not one more minute!*
and her child, stealing another minute.

If you stepped toward the shimmering
instead! Eighteen million more minutes. Approximately.

You were loved. On average. Tick tock.
Full of blood. In another minute you might see a girl in sandals

solemnly walking a golden lab. Might have seen. Shell toenail polish.
Plume wagging. Outside on the sidewalk. Your heart's not in it.

Dazzle of too much light. Later the sky
might break open with rain. Did. Rain all night.

The Doorbell

He said he had a cold and was going to bed,
then locked his door. I'd only been her lover
for a week. A smell entered the air
like mice enter cupboards,
sweet but brutal. She stood in the shared
hallway and called his name:
called to the empty room. Finally
the door surrendered to her shoulder.
So he was folded in death, thick banner of blood
on the bed and floor. The police were called,
the smell hurt so much that grief stayed away
after the body was taken. That night she sat in shock,
drinking to knock the smell from her throat.
For his parents, who would drive all night,
she hauled his mattress, heavy with blood,
to the alley's dumpster, scrubbed the damaged wood,
repaired what she could.

Hot August night. Bleach and despair,
oh despair: *the doorbell, doorbell,*
his mother and father climbed the spiral stair
to the third floor apartment in Outremont.
She guided them through the unhinged door,
open window blowing clean air from Mont Royal.
She watched them take in the stain on his medical texts,
his good shoes, swallow the scent of maculate wood,
breathe in the last trace of their son's blood.
She held his mother's arm and talked her through the nightmare
as she talks women through the worst kind of labor,
when the baby's died, but has yet to be born, and I saw
the toughness of her heart, the courage of her hands,
I put my life in them.

Fair

No fair, he says, when he learns
that his sister got a treat and he didn't. I even it out,
let them grow up a little without knowing the truth,
let them believe in fairies that collect teeth
and mothers with power to ward off grief.

If life were fair I'd watch the wand of impartiality
blast my neighborhood, pollute our water.
Malarial mosquitoes would drift
across lawns of houses once beautiful.
Fathers would walk three hours to work to save the fare.
Sons in my son's class would leave school to make bricks.
I'd mark my name with an illiterate X,
gather with other mothers to glean millet,
sell oranges, share our dreams of antiviral medication,
children who sleep without crying in hunger, a daughter
who has to sell herself for loaves and fishes.

But the same night in Peru:
baskets of tomatoes, fragrant beans.
In Bangladesh, small girls might put aside their coal sacks,
feel the clank of pocket money.
In rural China, eggs would gleam
in the kitchen of every house, and in the cities,
children would have brothers and sisters again.
In Burma, the golf courses of generals would be eaten
by locusts, and all the boys and girls
would find shoes on their feet. In North Korea,
a generation would grow three inches overnight.

In Iran, a girl named Neda would open her eyes, blood rushing back
into her whole heart, and many hands would help her to her feet,
call out, *God is Great! God is Great!*
In Sudan, a Zaghawa girl would rise,
eyes shining, holding her mother's hands, that had not, after all,

been hacked off by the Janjaweed after her rape.
She would be holding her mother's unblemished hands.
Someone would have seen that she had already borne
all she could withstand.

Sleep, darlings, in your illusions,
and let me sleep in mine, that against all evidence
reason will conquer monsters, nightmares endure
only a night's length, that we will be fair
to each other. In the green gardens
of childhood, crickets sing, even in the camps
song asserts itself like bubbles in porridge.

I will be your cradle, your chapel, your temple,
your truth and all you forget. Courage,
small mysteries! Who knows what will happen?

Wear your sweater, your charm, your mother's song.
Wear your ears and eyes. Remember Lorca,
in the green morning before he was shot,
wanted to be a heart.

Happy

1.

Once I caught a child who fell from the sky.

Now, as we live out the happily ever after,
I hold my breath. The children thrive,
each one a necessary chamber of the heart
waiting to be blown. Roulette.
All afternoon I watch my firstborn son flip
on the diving board: dark head, stone edge.

Tonight my daughter, mermaid hair floating ink
in the bath, cool and remote as she was before birth,
clad in foam, drifts away from childhood.
I run down the drain with the water.

Just like that, the baby opens the gate and runs
towards traffic, fat elbows pumping,
but I am still fast enough to dive for him.
Think quick! say the gods,
and toss us a life.

2.

Look, I tell them as we pass the woman
with broken teeth, the one we pass most Saturdays
either begging on her knees
or breathing the smoke of crystal
through a glass tube. *Don't get lost,*
don't stray, there are wolves out there.
Their eyes, clear water over black rocks, look past me.
They promise to be good,
to yes to no to never.

In the dark when she speaks French
time holds its breath,
but the door. The door.
The door is ajar.

When it comes I will say,
I've been waiting for you
the whole time I was happy.
I left the door open for you to come in
like Elijah at the feast.
Sometimes I dreamed you had forgotten me.

3.

Once I caught a falling child.
I left my own son wedged in a rubber swing.
As someone's toddler reached the edge between ledge
and forgotten ladder, I closed the gap. He stood
on tiptoe, launched.

I, who have dropped the keys, dropped the porcelain
vase, fumbled every ball thrown,
leapt to the sacred place
and opened my arms. The force
knocked us down. His soft hair brushed dust.
He wasn't mine, so I released him to rush
into the arms of a babysitter.

Her mouth shook as she thanked me,
lashed him to the stroller, fled.
All day he lived happily ever after.
I quaked like milk, brushed dust from my hips,
swallowed howls.

Wind spilled the fifth cup of wine,
blew the door closed.
I am the secret his mother won't dream.

Résumé of Failure

Born to a mother married to a man who was not
my father; failed to rid myself of his name. Failure at team
sports. Failure at Double Dutch. Failed
to get through a single year of school
without losing my coat. Failure to keep my friend
from drowning, my brothers from
felony, my parents from splitting. First failed
sobriety: age two at a party (culprit: beer)
though numerous hippies were also responsible.
Failure to fly, age six. Failed to keep his hands
off, age eleven. Failed virginity.
Failure to go into a store
without stealing something throughout the eighties.
Failure to impress a beautiful girl
by accidentally giving her father
an envelope of my and my boyfriend's pubic hair.
Ongoing failure to understand how such an act
could be accidental. (But it was.)
Failure to relax while drawing blood
from patients' hands. Failure at waiting
tables. Failed heterosexuality.
Failure at vegetarianism while dating
a vegan, fall 1997 (culprit: bacon).
Failure to give birth naturally. Failed VBAC.
Failure as a humanist
to know how to confront evil.
Failure to reconcile myself
to the horror. Failure to complete a single
sudoku. Failure to imagine my own death.
Failure to convince any of them to stay
alive. Failure to back up in darkness.
Failed hypnosis. Repeated failure
at prayer.

References available upon request.

What We Heard About Doctors

We heard they promised first
to do no harm. In medieval pain, crying out,

we gave them our bodies. But what they didn't know
hurt us. Their hands delivered germs

from the plague-ridden dead
to the womb of the woman in labor. They purged us,

transfused us with the blood
of goats. Still, they didn't leave us. They sat up nights,

a tightness in their throats, taking our pulse.
At cold midnight they dug up graves

to practice their strange arts,
relationship of liver, spleen, uterus and heart.

They spoke of bile, of tumors and ill winds.
They wrapped our boils in lint, anointed us with honey,

fastened leeches to our anemic skin, bled us,
fed us hot wine, tincture of cocaine.

If a limb grew gangrenous,
if cancer spread, they gave us whiskey,

whetted their knives.
If thy right eye

offend thee, pluck it out,
yes, they did this for us, to us.

We begged them to stitch us back to health
Who else would mend us? Who else

would speak with our husbands
when the beatings broke bones?

When we came with boils, burns,
they met our reluctant eyes. They put back our dropped

uteri. We made them strawberry pie,
thanked them for bad news.

We were infants in their hands,
wet and speechless. They turned us,

wiped us clean. Their eyes: wells of witness,
births and deaths drowned deep, were where we saw

the last reflection of ourselves
as we lay down to sleep.

What the Doctor Heard

Some guy lost a light bulb in his rectum
and expected me to find it. I did.

One smashed motorcycle, a girl with eyeballs popped
like stemmed grapes on her cheeks. A widower

who came by ambulance, wanted me to wash his ears
of wax now that his hands shake.

Don't complain to me about running late.
My wife has moved to the guest bed.

I parked illegally outside. My chest hurts.
I need to check if I signed off on the last chart.

I need to fart. How many times will you ask
if I can write a note for you to stay home from work

because you are sad? Will nothing slow the runoff
from your incontinent mouth? I'll write a note

if you'll go away. Purgatory: a waiting room
of comic tragedies. When your son came in

brain-dead, I made the call. I stood
with a clipboard while you cried

like a man gored by a bull.
I fought the urge to wait in the hall.

I put my hand on your shoulder, kept it there.
Once I believed I would actually do

no harm. Still you talk to me about this tingling
in your left hip after eating fish—what could it mean?

Don't seek trouble. When you hear hoofbeats, don't look
for zebras. My textbook case, we're part of each other's stories now.

Take off your uniform. Prepare yourself
for palpation. Probe, probe.

My body meets your body, vertical
against horizontal. We speak the spectacle.

I scrub for six happy birthdays, then turn,
both hands raised in surrender to meet your pain.

Waiting for the Biopsy Results

We don't talk about it. We put it out of mind.
It clings like mist, like cobweb, to our skin.
When I wake it presses, sticky, invisible,
and in that interlude I can't name the mood,
confuse the burst of anticipation with joy,
like waiting for a birth. Then the waiting names itself.
When the strange red poppy begins to bloom its fear
inside me, I refuse, I push back each petal to the hard
unbloomed green hat of the bud, the hat that women wear
when their hair falls out, I will not let it open its heart,
I will not take this flower until the call comes
and I must take this flower.

What We Heard About Death

We heard there is a white room, a long tunnel. Or maybe
a door. We heard that the stars bloom into supernovas

and a sudden scent of almonds and oranges
fills our mouths. Doves whir into the dying of the light

And we feel pure delight: all the mothers are there
arms outstretched, all the grandmothers, laps full of apples

and the children who died, even the miscarriages
we'd wept over, beckoning with translucent hands.

We heard there are angels,
forty virgins waiting to be deflowered,

that the rivers run milk
and the banks ooze honey.

We heard there is no such thing
as death, all life is an endless circle,

and we'll return as bodhisattva
or locusts consuming the field,

or perhaps as the field, heavy with longing,
each wheatberry trembling in its shaft.

That death's light is white,
is blue, is pure, death's peace, infinite. O ambrosia

night unscrolled in the shudder of harps.
Which star will we shatter,

plucked from the azure grip of the gods
who never answered our prayers?

Ash rising from a sunset of lemon groves, sati pyres,
from the blood-dipped paws of lions.

Beloved: we heard there was a scythe, grim
slice of last breath, last song flooding the lungs

and then would come the end of ends, the beginning
of beginnings, the silence of silences.

What Death Perhaps Heard

I heard you are afraid of me. That I have
many names among you, and none

among the animals whom you believe have
no souls, and whom you like to think

do not fear my arrival. But all fear my arrival
until I take them in my arms.

I am mother to many children, all crying out to me
at once, and they twist with longing,

they burn. In the end I come
with promises. I come

in the end, offering relief.
As for souls, what a lovely belief,

that spirit rises on the last breath
as a jellyfish lifts into the blue

light-pierced waters, opening and closing
its body, as bubbles float from the wishing wands

you give your children, and my cool arms
open and close like a lake.

Your temples are ethereal, yes,
your sonatas immortal. Praise you,

peacock's turquoise, praise you,
gazelle's pirouette, lion's padded step.

You can run from me your whole life,
or you can meditate on my inevitability:

I am indifferent. Pinworm and gorilla,
painted tortoise, giant clam,

baby in Sudan, baby in Saskatchewan:
You have my word. I will come.

Once my job was simple: you caught plague
or the baby's head got stuck

and I was there, in the midst of great pain.
I worked quickly among the humans and the animals

and then I gathered up my tools and left.
In tubercular coughs, in cholera,

in leprosy, in pneumonia, the hoof
of a horse, the field of a battle, you have known me.

Now when I turn the key, open the door,
lean to plug a throat, singing forth

the death rattle, you suction with tubes.
Now when the heart stops, you bypass

the heart. When the brain is dead,
you continue the foolish pulse and breath

of the body and think you've discovered something,
but you have discovered nothing.

No matter. I am your breast full of cancer,
water under bridges that crushes you when you jump.

I am your hangman's rope. I am the stones
in the desert and the mob that throws them.

I am the burning tire necklaced around your throat.
I am the silence after the truck is sucked to the bottom of the lake.

I am the pitch-change in the newborn's cry
that cry of recognition. Omega, that's me.

Like snowflakes, I come to each of you
precisely. Little ones, sweet chariots,

In Chinese opera you clench your hands
and throw back your head,

and that means me. I heard you are afraid
to be, or not to be.

Last Poem

Go, then, if you must. Go, if you are sure
you can stay no longer. Today an oncoming car
hit a spring-fool squirrel,

                                    shot of white brains splashed high,
tail slapping the street like a cowboy slaps his thigh
when the joke burns whiskey.

So much we can't avoid hitting head-on.

No, we're not here for any reason.
Who am I to say you should stay
and suffer your span of years
just so you won't make anyone cry
by choosing the date of your death?

I'd say go with my blessing, if I could.

All will continue, that's something: the earth
warming a little every year, polar bears
swimming further to meet the ice,
raccoons ticking across the deck
to scavenge our compost, and we'll put candles
in wine bottles to add solstice light.

We swerve when we can but we still cause damage.

But if you're not sure, if you're not sure,
wait a while. Let me sing to you a little
of the deer of the meadow
who jump their startled hightail,
whitetail the fence of summer's garden,
apple trees heavy with blossom.

Walk with me through the city in the morning
when mothers wear their new babies to cafés, raw

and open and the man without a roof
pushes his cart down Broadway
singing an aria from Carmen,
when a pigeon smacks the window
and a girl with green mittens
strokes its feathers as its eyes lose their light.

If you're not sure, if you're not sure,
you could wait out your grief another season.
You could change countries instead.
You could go to the library
and listen to tapes until you speak Italian.
You could get a dog from the pound and a truck to sleep in.
You could get clean from heroin, walk around pure
and empty as an envelope. You could sponsor a refugee family
to live with you for the next three years.
Though it might break your heart, it would also be useful,
and the opposite of lonely. Or you could finally leave him.
You could plant guerilla gardens in abandoned parking lots
and offer tomatoes to passers-by with both hands.
Your life could become the eccentric song,
the extravagant gesture, the red fruit freely given.
You could read to men in prison. Wouldn't you like to grow old
and see hair sprout in tufts from your ears?

Let your scars tell their story, but stay. Stay.
Look at your hands, inherited from your father,
your mother's peasant ankles,
the long lashes of your grandfather
who was a nobleman, who was a farmer.
You could have pity on yourself, as you would on any child
trapped in a burning building, you'd rush in to save her,
pressing her face to your coat until the air was safe.

You could press this poem over your face like a mask.

You could rip it out and make an origami crane.

You could put it in a bottle as a message
to a stranger. You could take it out,
read it as a stranger's answer.
If you're not sure, stay. Stay
at least until you put out
the love letter
on fire at your door.

Acknowledgements

Academic Pediatrics, "What We Heard About Doctors."

Bright Well, "Waiting for the Biopsy Results."

Clover, "The Opposite of War," "What the Heart Perhaps Heard" as "Heartsong," and "What We Heard About the Heart."

Contemporary Verse 2, "A Spectacle of Yourself" and "What We Heard About the Sea."

Event, "Drunk," and "Vancouver General" as "Delivery Room Under Renovations."

Fire on Her Tongue, "The Opposite of War" and "Waiting for the Biopsy Results."

Prairie Fire, "Mother and Dogs."

Rattle, "What We Heard About the Americans" and "What We Heard About the Canadians."

Rhythm, "Daphne to Peneus."

Rocksalt: An Anthology of Contemporary B.C. Poetry, "What the Sea Perhaps Heard."

The Alaska Quarterly Review, "Ablution."

The Atlanta Review, "What Death Perhaps Heard," which was also performed by Heather Pawsey, soprano, at The Western Front, November 2011, and "What We Heard About Death."

The Briar Cliff Review, "What the Suicide Can't Hear."

The Malahat Review, "Aubade: Grendel's Mother," "Maternal Sapphics I," "The Willingness to Be Wounded" as "Willingness," and "Uncut Wood."

Through an Open Door, "I Might Be Nothing" as "I Might Be Nothing (Lara's Song)."

I gratefully acknowledge the Canada Council and the BC Arts Council for grants that gave me time to write. My thanks to the following people: Rhea Tregebov, who loaned me her quiet office, and has always given me personal and poetic support at the right times; Kara Stanley and Simon Paradis, who gave me friendship, music, inspiration, and courage; Susan Olding, Fiona Lam, Jane Silcott, and Judy McFarlane, for the Jericho beach walks, for being available to take a look, for the support that only writers can offer writers. Sam Green has been my teacher for thirty years; nobody I know has so fully offered himself up to poetry, and to poets; thank you, Sam. Thank you, Bryan Miller, for the place in Brooklyn, for sending poems my way, for your careful ear. Leslie Uyeda has brought music to my poems and my life. Louise Hager loves books and loves connecting people—we all benefit. Lorna Crozier's great poetry and great generosity are true gifts. Wayne Koestenbaum provokes and inspires; thank you. I thank my parents, Mary Rose, Bob Rose, Jim Prier and Shelley Mason, for reading to me. I thank my brother, Jefferson Rose, for the musical collaboration, and for talking me down when the life of an artist gets rough. My children, Benjamin, Gabriele and Thomas, are their own poems. Isabelle Fieschi, my love for nearly twenty years now— thank you for being steadfast and true. You are my first reader, my compass and my anchor, feast and song.

Notes

The *pas de deux* is a poetic form I created in 2004. This form consists of a pair of poems that analyze and debate a subject. It allows for opposing and contradictory points of view, and supports a multiplicity of voices. In art, this form would be a collage; in science, a symposium; in tragedy, a Greek chorus; in philosophy, a dialectic, and in dance, a *pas de deux*.

"What We Heard About Rain" evokes Heraclitus' famous dictum, "No man ever steps in the same river twice."

"Hymn to Shit": With apologies to Basho and T.S. Eliot.

"What We Heard About Death" ends with a line from Hamlet's soliloquy, "To be, or not to be."

Rachel Rose is a writer whose work has appeared in journals in Canada, the US, New Zealand and Japan. Her first book, *Giving My Body to Science* (McGill/Queen's University Press, 1999) was a finalist for the Gerald Lampert Award, the Pat Lowther Award and the Grand Prix du Livre de Montreal, and won the Quebec Writers' Federation A.M. Klein Award. Her second book, *Notes on Arrival and Departure*, was published by McClelland & Stewart in 2005. Winner of the Peterson Memorial Prize for poetry and the Bronwen Wallace award for fiction, she holds a BA in English from McGill University and a MFA in Creative Writing from the University of British Columbia. She lives in Vancouver, BC.